The Dragon of Sassafras Mountain
and
Other Poems

Seth Steinzor

Fomite
Burlington, VT

ISBN-13: 978-1-959984-60-3
Library of Congress Control Number: requested

Fomite
58 Peru Street
Burlington, VT 05401
www.fomitepress.com
05-03-2024

Contents

Dedicated to Grandma Ida

Call this a "found poem." It is pretty much verbatim what I overheard.

Woman Overheard Talking on Cell Phone, Summer 2018

Where you sleepin' tonight?
Where you sleepin' tonight?
If I knew where to find you
I think that it would be alright.

I'm here at the Walmart.
I'm here at the Walmart.
I got a cart full of stuff.
It's much too hot for sleepin' rough.

I'll go to the shelter.
I'll go to the shelter.
If I knew where to find you...
It's much too hot for sleepin' rough.

I wrote this poem at the request of a dear friend, the wife of a dear friend. He was recovering from cancer surgery. She was bedridden with cancer. I visited them for a couple of weeks to care for them. While I was there, she asked me to write her eulogy. The day after I left, she entered hospice.

Now It Is Finished
(for Jane Courtney Weed 6/12/1949 - 9/1/2012)

Now it is finished
and you have stopped withdrawing
into a self that cannot be found anywhere

now the pink bathrobe
is uninhabited like the body
and the clear plastic tubes that fed you
enriched air these last months are discarded

now your lips have pursed
the last time on sweetness and tartness
and the last laugh has left your belly

now memories grow uncertain
as cigarette smoke and
piercing as the tang of wine that
hovers above the empty goblet

we will carry you

when we asked you about the afterlife
you said "remains to be seen"

and I think you might have laughed
had somebody said
"we don't want to know about the remains
we want to know about what's unseen"

I can hear you laughing
in all its charming variety your laughter

of all of us who knew you
who cannot hear it

you hired a doctor to give you the right poisons
you hired a nurse to care skillfully
you asked a poet to find words for when it's done

here's what's carved on Billy Butler Yeats' stone:
      Cast a cold eye
      On Life, on Death.
      Horseman, pass by!
and here's what Rilke composed for himself:
      Rose, oh pure contradiction,
      Joy of being. No-one's sleep
      under so many lids
and here's what you thoughtfully said:
      it's very important to be nice

polite, certainly
never consciously unkind
plenty - perhaps a bit too much - of turn the other cheek

but not the smiling lying kind of niceness
nor namby pamby, no:
the kind of niceness that is stamped in steel

you tended each of your dying parents with desperate assiduity
sacrificing peace of mind, health, livelihood,
and truth be told
      (a Jane phrase - *truth be told* -
      I think it in your voice)
                  a certain amount of marital harmony
to ensure that through that long subtractive process

which ends with everything lacking and nothing wanted
no day would be empty of attentive loving
   because it's what people do, dammit

your face heart-shaped
your mouth small and potentially prim
but it was so often merry
   I don't mean "glad" or "happy," I mean "merry"
     as in Dickens certain characters - Fezziwig, for example
     or the Cheeryble brothers - are merry
   the easy overflow of a generous heart

Damariscotta girl, your husband denominated you
something to do with whitewashed mullions
seawashed granite
knowledge of which fork and where to put it
the unyielding kernel of humanity
wrapped in just the right shade of social exchange

before I met you, a union activist
a labor leader a contract negotiator
imagine facing across the conference room table
that politely intransigent reasonableness

when we met, you had restrung your bow
to play a rather different sort of chamber music

   admirer of formal British gardens
   collector of McCoy Pottery
interior designer - that is one who makes
order and harmony
aesthetically pleasing and life enhancing

   (didn't you wince a little when
   we hung the plastic tubes from the trim
   over your bed in the parlor to which
   your world had narrowed to see the

open eye screw pierce the fine white
glossy paint job Mr. Lou did for you
- never a drip - long ago)

    and when the design business went bust
librarian - no profession more evocative of
just how close we poor animals can come to
giving some part of ourselves to life eternal and
how delicate the leaves in which we preserve it
- *ssh* -

your vices were the costs of your virtues

a tendency to become overwhelmed and frustrated
consequent upon the unremitting unconscious effort
to be what you should be and do what you should do

a certain waspishness when overwhelmed or frustrated
at the unaccountable recalcitrance of things and people
to be what they should be and do what they should do

    (not to imply that you were unworldly
    to the contrary, you down-to-earth down-easter,
    bewildered not that badness exists but by its stupidity)

a sometimes resort to the grape
for relief from knowing how inevitably
we must fall short

    if only by leaving before those we leave are ready for it

an immoderate taste for televised British mysteries
in which evil however clever is rooted out by
understated mildly emotionally repressed
clear thinking keen observation and humane values

    NOW

how ironic that the thing which at last would lay you low
       most civilized of persons
       full of all the civilized decencies
       attached to civility like a mussel to a boulder
              (as Thomas More was attached to the law, because
              what else will stand between you and the devil)

how ironic that what took you from us
was a few cells throwing off the compact
whereby the body's constituent parts agree to respect their mutual
roles and places in the service of long and amicable coexistence
and in riotous anarchy bringing the whole house down

sweet and kind and loving to the end
if everyone were like you, there'd be no more war
and we'd all have nicer homes

High School Class of '70 Junior Year Final Exams

1.

Number two pencils
race everywhere but here; at
this desk, time has stopped.

2.

Should I go back and
erase all the black dots I
wasn't sure about?

3.

That curly strand of
hair that brushes that girl's neck
has all the answers.

4.

Clocks that sleepily
tocked through classes now tick tick
tickticktickticktick.

5.

I was the first to
put my pencil down and leave.
Nobody else looked up.

6.

Everybody else
I talked to got something else
for number eighteen.

Five-Year-Old Wins Fishing Derby

All of a sudden, there was a weight where there wasn't

any before, and she pulled, remembering to reel
most of the time, the steelhead's balky bulk out
of the water, up the bank, to her feet.
Its silver, breaking out from the blurry green below,
stood out sharply, many hued as the pebbly dirt.
Her eyes never left that place it peeled out of
endlessly, grudgingly leaving its world for hers.

Later, someone photographed the little girl,

caught her with her catch for the news: elbows bent
wide, she hoists it to smear her yellow jumper,
jaws to chest, belly to belly, tail curled
because the ground's not low enough, it can't
hang straight. The cameraman's laughter
shook his frame, but she, blonde cub, bore
her eleven pounds of cold grey unsmiling.

Emily Dickinson

In that less populous time - fewer like you.
To meet a kindred spirit - even to tap
spirit messages across the walls of matrimony -
set joy to flutter against gratitude's cork
like a butterfly in a bottle.

The wonder is not that you were immured.
You would have been - whatever you did.
The wonder is how - so firmly knowing
walls for walls - you chose your own
over l'amour, laudanum, or "the vapors."

Your delight in basic things - and steady
gaze on what stirs in the dusty corner -
show a lifer accepting her sentence -
studying the barred light from all angles,
nourishing herself on bits of lettuce.

In the latter nineteenth century, the Eddy brothers held seances in their house in Pittsford, Vermont. They became so famous that a prominent journalist, Col. Henry S. Olcott, visited them to investigate as thoroughly as he could whether he could debunk them.

Echoes of the Eddys

We are pusillanimous in the face of ghosts.
Think of that woman at Tanglewood, too seized up
to scream that summer afternoon in the hallway
when her hair, hanging limply on her neck, was brushed
swiftly across one shoulder and then the other
by unseen hands. Later, she said it was like a
playfully affectionate child, and innocent;
but no way would she spend the night in that house, no.
Her companions, though untouched, had abandoned her.
They ran. I never have felt my hackles rise
except in thinking of such things, mere thinking of
the dark figure that waits on the couch beside me,
the hand that may reach from behind to stroke my cheek.
Then I read Colonel Olcott's account of doings
a hundred years ago in Vermont, upstairs at
the Eddy brothers' ramshackle farmhouse where he
and many other guests lodged - ate and slept - for weeks.
The ghosts they'd come to meet there had cold, sweaty skin.
A woman passed her hand beneath one's shirt, and ran
fingertips across breasts she said swelled chill and damp
as ocean waves. To Olcott's disappointment, he
never was allowed to dance with that spirit, a
gay, lively squaw called Honto, although others were;
also, the room was too dark to make out faces;
also, he wasn't allowed in the chamber where
William Eddy sat alone, summoning dozens
of humanly shaped shades each night but Sunday to
brief visits with audiences of dozens of
the quick. Once, weakening before she could pass back

through the sole, curtained door to William's cubicle,
Honto sank to her waist in the floor, laughed, and slid
to the drape like a footless chess piece. Pawn or queen?
Sustained at first by skepticism, Olcott measured
rooms, sealed windows with gauze and wax, swished back cobwebs
in dusty attics, sought trapdoors and costume trunks
without success, counted the cast of characters,
painted scales to record the apparitions' heights
(from two-and-a-half feet to a bit over six)
and hauled in scales to weigh them (Honto averaged
sixty pounds or so, but fluctuated wildly).
At last he was reduced, like the newly bereft
mothers who came to wail at one last vision of
babies doubly torn from the body, to belief
at once grudging and enthusiastic. "Wonders,"
he called them, beyond his powers to explain or
more than describe. He recounted but one stab of
fear: sitting in the loft's blackness, they felt beams shake
that were trees when the land belonged to those who now
danced, stomping and whooping among the silent chairs.
(No, two: an elderly woman, Honto's willing
partner in most hijinks, scrambled atop her seat
to escape a mouse that Honto let skitter loose.)
But when Olcott, having formed an unspoken wish,
felt it answered by the lips of a child he knew
to be dead softly kissing his face, there was none,
no more than the *frisson* of hope unexpectedly
blossoming. We can't bear such breathless affection,
we, in whose days corpses are bulldozed to mass graves
and not allowed to linger for farewells at home.

Who is S.S. Fishman?

He is someone wearing a yarmulke alone.
    He pulls the skullcap over his baldness
        the way Dr. Frankenstein in the movies
           helmets his golem
                preparing to give it life.
    This ritual completed, he
        may muse on the Shekhinah, Rebecca
           at the well - he laughs - *Gertrude,*
        long lost Gertrude, watering camels!
           The satin dome, so lightly pressing,
                filters much of the widower's pain.

He stayed in their white-walled New England
    Congregationalist town.
        Down valley, the French Catholics'
           skinny kids greet him from their bikes,
                "Hi, rabbi." That word he's taught them.
    Outskirting fields, like a green plate,
        hold houses like slices of Wonder Bread
           except for the gaudy French and his
        little pumpernickel house, its
           blackened and russet cedar shakes
                immured in greyish hedges.

Were there children? The one who died. The two
    who visit from respective coasts.
        When they turn their faces to him,
           it is as intermittently and distantly
                warming as November sunlight.
    He looks to the local kids'
        unhostile familiarity
           for the daily blessing it contains,
        to the local parents'
           mostly unhostile familiarity
                for the same, hidden berakha.

He dons his yarmulke, harkens to his g-d,
    and writes what he hears
        of the secret order of things:
            a g-d like Spinoza's but with a voice
                that sounds whole chords at once.
    There are vibrations that are sound,
        that beyond that are color,
            that beyond that are Sephiroth.
    These he attempts to transcribe,
        an old man with failing senses.
            Of course, something is lost.

"My home is my shtetl." This joke -
    did someone speak it?
        Back of the lilacs is a grassy hill
            like a breast with a stone nipple
                he climbs and sits on Shabbos noons,
  spring, summer, and fall, on that mound
        bared of the surrounding woods.
            Tree trunks like an organ's pipes
        he listens to, the soft whoosh
            and crackle accompanied
                by no voice but his.

Scene From My Youth

wee hours parking lot
empty pizza box tossed flops
open cop siren

The Cleanup Crew

tan and brown heap - two
bedraggled black birds squabble,
pick at spots of pink

March 23, 2001

where yesterday's birds
chirped by the curb, I find piled
the snow plow's present

Untitled

crust of gunk clogs choke
near driveway's bottom berm kills
blower still as snow

Okay, so this trope was perfected by Matsuo Bassho over three hundred years ago. His haiku has been variously translated. My favorite version is by Alan Watts:

> The old pond,
> A frog jumps in:
> Plop!

But just because something has been done perfectly once, doesn't mean we shouldn't try to do it again. How else can literature continue to live with us? So:

> Oh! Fish holds there, hooked,
> pulling hard... he won't move... he
> shakes his head... he's gone!

Shopping in the Time of Covid

worried I'll be caught
by what nips the herd's fringe I
quickly paw through fruits

Fighter Jets

air tears as they pass
and pushing loudly back fills
the vacuum they leave

Across the East River, Viewed From 42d Street

squalid angular
dun cityscape blue mist veils
but has not softened

Long Trail Summer (Mass. to Rte. 125)

After climbing rocks,
trail flattens. Minutes later,
I breathe through my nose.

*

Hiker, funk lost in
acres of mid-day sweetly
baking ferns, snoozes.

*

I squeeze water through
a ceramic filter. Then
I squeeze it through me.

*

driven drops sheet skin
sweet cool shiver streaming path
splashes oh thunder!

*

Deerflies bedevil.
Ticks lurk. Mossy stones slip. The
trail goes up and down.

*

The ego rides the
body like a mahout rides
a bull elephant.

Across the Parking Lot From My Office

salmon pink brick wall
contains parked cars' owners in
rows of blank windows

nothing moves except
sun's glint sliding from chrome trim
to side view mirror

from somewhere unseen
engines' gritty hum carries
floating birdsong chimes

Trip to Austin, Texas

Before departure - Saturday 4/1/00 7:30 a.m.

gulls' caws, bird songs drift
past roofs of rows of sleeping
houses, empty streets

First leg of the trip - Saturday 4/1/00 2:55 p.m.

jounce jounce - ah! a hard
bounce - alone in the aisle, the
flight attendant smiles

Dinner in Newark - Saturday 4/1/00 5:05 p.m.

they call this chicken
with string beans - a handsome man
sweeps the shiny floor

On the runway - Saturday 4/1/00 6:30 p.m.

"is Texas high in
the sky? - I made the plane stop,
I think" - "shush, Helen"

Sixth Street, Austin - Saturday 4/1/00 about midnight

bars blast noise - a girl
bends over, sheltering her
cleavage from the rain

Austin Omni Hotel - Sunday 4/2/00 8:15 a.m.

hotel room rings with
Xtian call to prayer - shower
dimly lit, tepid

LBJ Library - Sunday 4/2/00 11:00 a.m.

meat red document
boxes shelved 'twixt white stone walls
memory sandwich

LBJ Library - Sunday 4/2/00 11:30 a.m.

a winter's tender
thoughts of barefoot Tex-Mex kids,
then bombed the jungles

Artz Rib House - Monday 4/3/00 about 8:00 p.m.

the usual sides
and ribs while a trio serves
Floyd Tillman's tunes

Congress Ave. Bridge - Tuesday 4/4/00 about 8:15 p.m.

tourists line the rails
for the thick rope of bats that
streams from underneath

During the school year 1967-68, my father, a college professor, led a junior year abroad program in Italy. My family lived in Siena. I spent weekends with them. Monday through Friday, I stayed in a small hotel and attended school in Florence. It was a year full of the ecstasy and pain of sudden liberty. Much more of the former than the latter, actually. Fifty years later, I returned to the same hotel - possibly the same room.

Nel Cuore della Città

where I erupted age fifteen
fifty years ago
here now

drenched in honeyed evening light

flocks of east Asians
bristle with selfie sticks

a fat German guy and his
wife or girlfriend or daughter
queue up for doner kabob

Rumanians, French, English

at the least hint of rain
tall skinny black men
pop out as if from nowhere
hawking cheap umbrellas

there didn't used to be to pizza here
except on sheet trays in bars
little rectangular after-school snacks

now storefront signs all over

sport crudely drawn
round red pies and yellow spaghetti tangles

hollowed out movie set theme park

corpse dressed in the clothes it was wearing
coffin full of coins

barely furnished room I lived in

German twenty-somethings
party hearty across the courtyard

the dapper little hotelier
in his white suit and snappy white fedora
doesn't care for Arabs
I have just enough Italian
to understand and not respond

I stand in line three hours
where there were no lines

this dead end hall
dead Romans' busts commanded
when it was empty and dusty
opens now before it ends

to the side a big attraction
siphons crowds

away from the disregarded regiment

and the cul de sac where
poor Laocoön his sons and the
serpent perpetually struggle

In Ireland's Galway Bay is the tiny island of Inisheer, and on that island is a tiny, partly ruined, partly restored church that was built over a thousand years ago by the hardscrabble islanders. Over the ages it was covered by wind-blown sand but has been excavated. You can walk right in.

Teampall Chaomhàn, Inis Oirr

Winter would have disassembled you its
waters swelling in your joints and cracks to
pry you rock from rock to flake you if it
ever froze their richest offerings the
stench of rotting seaweed piled on limestone
making soil they made their living from the
net they cast of stones to hold it down and
shelter cattle from the winds the air they
opened up your roofless walls and floor to
digging out the sands the ocean's gales had
drifted over saving you perhaps from
ending a paddock hidden by the weather
from the weather never to be repaired and
never more a refuge from their lives

On Tully Mountain

A thousand feet above the bay
a wind that kept its hand in the pocket where the knife was
and this being Connemara those grey humpy beasts all over the sky
four-sided concrete column about waist high
with a surveyor's brass plate on top
rising at the summit out of a mound of quartzite shards
to which I'd added my one
now I leaned against it facing the wind like a reader at a lectern
the bay opened out below me
Crump Island flashed from olive drab to emerald
on it an abandoned church I knew, but could not see
the sea around the island came alive and
soon the whole bay glittered bluely
soon also the oil-paint stolidity of
Renvyle Point had exchanged for pastels
Rusheenduff Lake as vivid as a caste mark
and who remembered chiaroscuro when pointillism was all the rage
and after a while the sun rested its foot on my back
and massaged my shoulders with its toes
but the wind still kept its hand in its pocket
the grey humpies flowed back in and mottled and dimmed
everything the Bens across the valley
behind me lost their playful bubbling upthrust
cloaked once again in massive mysterious bare-headed dignity
and if they'd had hair the wind would have teased it
saying come on lover when it gets dark come to my room
so I headed back down the spongy heathered slopes to Derryinver
past the occasional black crescent gashes
where the turf had slumped from itself
and the crisscrossing sheep's paths, thin black and straight
down to that spicy thick perfume of
thousands of years being burned to warm the present
ah, the slow, slow deaths
where the pain is stretched so thin you can't feel it

those are among the best, and they give off a fine, peaty smell
now for a bowl of chowder and some tea

Terra Incognita: New Orleans 2010

You could come to visit and you would never know.
Mandina's waiters lace your turtle soup with sherry;
black-garbed pilgrims converge dry shod on the Superdome;
St. Charles' live oaks stretch gnarly branches impossible lengths;
on Bourbon, crowds rejoice in drinking until they puke;
a trombone's spit valve wets the pavement of Jackson Square;
Faubourg Marigny delights in home improvements;
freshly painted trim brightens Elysian Fields;
no watermarks on Desire, unless you already know.

*

But you can't find a map that shows the city whole.
The maps for tourists show only where tourists are wanted.
You point to one that hangs on the wall at the official
tourist info place, framed like a Degas, and say
you want a map just like it. The bored official tourist
info lady says they're out of print a long time,
since the storm at least, no idea why.
At last, at the other tourist info place,
they sell you a brochure containing several major
fragments of the city, unassembled, and dangling
off the side of one of these delicate grids of streets a
featureless grey blob labeled "Lower Ninth Ward."

*

Attempting to fill that space, you cross the St. Claude bridge
and ride a bike down Flood, down Florida's empty length,
and through the emerging savannah cartography's given up on.
Street signs echo street names spray painted on telephone poles.
White-shirted mostly black kids romp in a schoolyard's kraal,
a spot of brightness and noise surrounded by quiet absences.

On many blocks, the curbs are overgrown, the street runs
ragged as if drawn by a toddler in crayon green
for encroaching grass. One block, the curbs are clean and straight,
five houses in a row with glass not plywood windows.
A dog leaves its owner's weeds and chases you to the corner,
where the grass grows tall.

                                              His barking long behind,
you pass a habitation where a woman watches
from her lonely stoop, and you wonder, does she
ache like a phantom limb struggling to grow back?
You ride through acres of grass that rustles overhead.
A sign: "We cut tall grass." There's work enough, you think,
but where are all the workers? Hot breeze. The grass says, "Ssh."

                          *

You ask the clerk at the hotel, a dour, white-haired
woman, who says no map is to be had that shows the
city whole. "They're out of print for years." You say,
"It couldn't be the storm changed the streets." She pauses.
She says, "Oh yes, it did. Our streets were swimming pools.
Unless you were here, you can't imagine how it was."

In Waterbury, Vermont, After Irene

1.

I saw what flickered in the young mother's face -
she was not going to cry, at least not right away -
amid a cluster of kids head-droopingly bored but
too anxious to wander and anyway forbidden.
The former volunteer fireman pleaded with her
not to let the work crew back in her basement
until fans had been placed to dispel the fumes.
Like me, he'd just walked by, looking to help.
A teenage crew member said to me, "But oil
don't burn." I said, "You drop a match in a bucket
of oil and it'll go out. It's fumes that burn.
You don't want to come out of there in flames."
They'd been hacking up shelving and hauling it out,
having fun with sawzalls. I took the pieces and
wheelbarrowed them over to the dumpster, dull
green plank chunks dusted with golden sawdust
flecks that had stuck in the flood's residual slime.

2.

At a house not far from there, I saw a man
attack with vicious blows of a framing hammer the
underlayment in what had been his kitchen.
We'd scraped loose the vinyl tiles, tossed them
into heavy-duty plastic bags, and
humped them out to the dumpster, past the mound of
grey, crumbled drywall, pink fluffs of
fiberglass, dismantled cabinets, shards of
wainscoting taking up the whole front yard and
growing sodden there. Whoever had tacked that
plywood down, had not spared the nails. Our little
prybars and catspaws groaned it up slowly. It bent,

its stiffness soaked away, without the strength to
overcome the flooring boards' swollen grip.
Wordlessly, he picked up the claw and went at it,
splintering, splitting, smashing, swift and ferocious.
I stood back. His father said, "I told the
builder, build it like you were going to live here."

3.

I saw the house's innards, the hues of road kill,
grey and pink and brown on the lawn in the rain.
We loaded a plastic tub and the working wheelbarrow
handful by leather-gloved handful, globs of wallboard
decomposing to gypsum and paper, spears of
lath and molding spiked with nails, drawer parts,
shelving paper checkered blue and white,
clots of insulation the color of sunsets.
Trudging back and forth a couple of hours,
having reduced the pile perhaps by half,
we'd paused to catch our breath when someone vaguely
known to the family drove up in his bright blue
bucket loader. Soon he'd scooped the yard clear.
No one regretted our efforts, though they'd been useless.
A few blades of grass streaked the mud,
all lying in one direction, like a comb-over.
"I think you're going to have to reseed," I said.

Lathe Haiku

whirling chunk of wood
I caress with sharp steel peels
down to hidden blooms

Ambrosia Maple

brown clouds streak creamy
maple slab sawn open to
window's pale cold light

Spindle Turning

Brute force whirls
wood onto steel
applied with precise
intent and a light touch
to peel away ghosts

down to a round
spindle on which desires
registered with precise
intent and a light touch
manifest themselves.

The Difference Between Black Tea and Green Tea

Unfurling on the tongue, a fullness made
of many depths and points of shade:
assams reveal themselves in water.

Those flavors water shyly, pale, endues,
pi lo chun accents their hues:
a mother dressed up by her daughter.

Exotics

for Susan Weiss, lapsed vegan

In southern China
they eat civet cats, roasted whole and
braised in soy and hoisin sauce to hide the
gamey taste. The civet lives on durian, a
spiky fruit, foul-smelling, with a flesh as
subtle as the custard dreams are made of.

On North Street, Burlington, Vermont
near the oriental grocery stores,
expatriate Africans sick for home may find,
neatly piled on a tiny shop's back shelves where
stray Vermonters are unlikely to venture,
zip-locked bags of dried grubs, hard tan curls in
assorted sizes, but when I approach the clerk to
ask how are they cooked, I chicken out and
buy instead a round brown deep-fried thing that
disappointingly tastes just like a doughnut.

In Minnesota
tales of famous family Friday night
spaghetti dinners regaled the worldly Yankee
sophistication of a friend of mine whose own
family's odyssey had landed him in high school
far from maple sugar and cider doughnuts
there among the pines and walleye pike.
At last one evening he found himself seated among
half a dozen scions of Scandinavia
logger-large and hunching over shining
formica, facing a bowl of palely gleaming,
naked noodles, and a bottle of ketchup.

Indonesia
original home of the scarlet condiment's forebears.

In New York
Brooklyn, to be precise, my newly-wed mother
scandalized her husband and parents-in-law by
pouring ketchup on her scrambled eggs, an
act so odd that even the rubric "goyish"
couldn't encompass it; but she was from
Chicago, so what could you expect? And I
have taught my children to follow the same strange ways.

In America
they'll heap anything - bacon and cheese, whatever -
onto baked goods ubiquitously sold as "bagels"
that are neither dense nor chewy; fine-grained
bready toroids with the crust removed and a
shiny glaze engineered in its place. Those, and
hand-coiled rings purportedly *en manière de
Montreal*, sweeter and maltier than anything
I remember, are all you can get around here. But

In Buffalo, New York, 1960
Mastman's redolent deli, full of derma
stuffed with kasha, knishes, pickled herring,
smoked whitefish, lox - "the real nova" - and
bins of "Jewish hockey pucks," just plain or
pumpernickel, forged of fully developed
gluten, steam, and fire, as heavy as history,
yielding to the teeth like summer to fall
(in those days, gradually), holding warmth but
autumnally flavored, bagged by the dozen or one
"with a schmear" of cream cheese impasto slapped on by
mustachioed Mastman himself, unobtainable now,
rarer than civet cats with their strong sauces,
digested and carried into internal exile.

September 11, 2001

The airplane whacks the building, the orange
fireballs billow and roil, the black specks sprout
arms and legs as they fall faster, the white
cloud obscures but cannot hide the structure
collapsing onto its inhabitants.
Over and over.

                    May those who planned this
be devoured by those who would devour them.
They have given themselves over to that.
I also piously wish that those who
devour them may choke on it. I can find
nothing to hope for that does not mock my
hope: a smiley face drawn in soot, a thumb
black with pulling a curving mouth and two
dotted eyes clean, encircled on a shard.

Nine Eleven, Oh! Too

There are those who really lost
something that can be lost, but
they are not the ones who say,
"Everything has changed," not
those who look back on the date
and remember where they were
when the horrid pictures flashed
and interrupted what they
were doing and would resume.

There is an instant before
you die that you can practice
to be ready for, empty
of thought, when all you see is
what is. Those whose names are squashed
beneath hundreds of stories
rolled through printing presses and
broadcast to the winds had no
chance to love that empty chance

before the floors suddenly
fell from them and on them.
Fearful little men running
from the blaze now run us. They
have made a banner of the
date and wave it blindingly,
three numbers on yellow cloth
as thin as scraped skin, while you,
who have lost nothing, make the
noises that you think you should.

"Curtains Ordered for Media Coverage of Returning Coffins"
(Washington Post, October 21, 2003)

Your commanders sneak your
unanticipated bodies home
for burial with purely local
ceremony - words, a moment of
silence, a troubled face on a
singular front page that disappears
quicker than acne - young soldiers,

so that the national mirror,
history's first draft, may show
nothing less clear and untroubled
than the doings of Ben and J.Lo.

And if tranquility's stalked by
shadows, a second sense that
something's forgotten, well, let us
remind you, someone somewhere
else - two gay men kissing,
an abortionist, a terrorist's gaudy
sideshow - see what you're missing?

After the Fall

The world will not miss us.
Absent the phantom pastels of maps,
the continents will break
what the sun alone pours
into billions of vivid splashes.
Plenty will shake the air long after
the echoes of Elizabeth Bishop
singing that word "maps"
dissipate in the general molecular whirl.

A cold time will come, and a time of rains.
Much will cease before the sky
clears blue and blank as a baby's eye,
then turns puffy with random squalls,
every morning and evening bloodshot,
flags of red that signal nothing but
themselves, their flaring, fading moment.
Truly, there will be no ideas but in things.

All verse will be unmeasured and blank:
stones' slow, guttural epics
alongside, above, and under
hissing, volatile lyrics of streams;
lilting couplets of insects, birds,
animals, and fish; vast sonnets
of vegetable love; oceans' massive mutter.
The world will not miss us.

The world will not miss us.
Vines will wind among the trees
untrained by any Miltonic gardeners.
Beetles striped yellow and brown
will eat wild food and no one's pickles.
If dogs and cats survive their masters,

their whelps and kittens will erase
the dim line between feral and domestic.

There will be no ruins, no vermin, only
cockroaches and rats at play in the
interesting new jumble. No one,
sweating through the noon's higher heat,
will recall what I now recall: a boy,
restless at midnight, trolling for
visions through a mumbling window
of his sleeping family's home,

startled by a sudden, white glare.
It throws him off the couch cushions
to his feet, tensed for flight, laughing
to see it's a car, not a bomb. Since then,
two children have come to me,
eight new limbs They may cut off.
Every day, I watch my children's growing
awareness of what careens this way.
The world will not miss us.

We were seventeen.

In Her Room

I solemnly lowered the zipper from her neck
to just below her breasts. She lay there quietly,
her eyes intent on my face, her lower lip
(with that upturned crescent of scar, a pale
moon, just beneath it, I found so endearing)
gently sucked between her teeth, so I
ventured to lower it to her navel, slowly,
receiving neither protest nor approval.
She could have shrugged her arms out of
the jumpsuit's sleeves just then, but she did not:
she lay there quietly, her eyes intent on my face,
her lower lip (with that upturned crescent
of scar, a pale moon, just beneath it,
I found so endearing) gently sucked
between her teeth, so I slipped my right hand
under the blue fabric that felt thick and warm,
under her breast, which one didn't matter,
she lay quietly, intent, her lower lip
released, neither protesting nor welcoming.
I slid my hand up the flaccid mound to its
hard tip that I knew from other times I'd
peeled the fabric back was chocolate brown,
and rested there, it in my palm, her lower
lip once more between her teeth, her eyes
intent but inward as if having taken in
my face now she took it all the way in.
My hand rode the velvet of her steady
beathing up and down, then down and
down the ribs rising and falling, past
flatness and rested over the well of her
navel that thrilled my palm as her nipple had.
Still she lay still. A wildness had entered

her face, not resisting nor urging, so I
followed the slope of her belly down
to where the down thickened to a
scratchy underthicket and the band of her
underpants held and pressed my fingers
the way her hand had held and pressed them
on her cheek just eternities ago, and under
that was skin folded and wrinkled as I
could not imagine, moist and warm as her
tongue. Just then her mother rattled pots
downstairs in the kitchen and I withdrew
my fingers slick with lovely musk, and ever
after, her zipper carefully, soundlessly drawn,
mystery had new dimensions and layers.

To a Former Lover

In my dream, and a short while after awakening,
I could not remember your name.
I remembered the turrets of your nipples
atop your slackened breasts the day you lay
dozing on the rocks high above the quarry
where people swam, that day we first met.
I remembered the complex curves of your abdomen,
a concavity running each side of your convex belly,
the ridges and peaks of your hips cradling
your gingery thatch, and the years I wandered in those hills,
first in joy and then sometimes in desperation.
I remembered your snaggle-toothed grin and your
googly eyes that seemed to me and still seem to me
beautiful, and I remembered your decision,
gratefully ratified, to abort our child.

I remembered so much - our fights and of course
what followed them; your passionate intelligence;
the day I came to live in your town and you
inscrutably turned your back on me; your shoulder blades
sharp as knives or wings, square as cinder blocks;
part of your chest brushing part of my chest when you
slowly turned back to me, crying - but
I could not remember your name.
To each memory, I could not put a name.
I told myself each time that even so, missing only
a set of syllables meaningless in itself, I still held
the better part of whatever I could ever hold of you;
and then by straining to call your name, helpless
not to, as helpless as not to take a breath,
I cursed the sky and the worms that devour us.

The last line of this poem is something my mother said to a family gathering one Thanksgiving towards the end of her life. I've been mulling it over ever since.

Yesterday, While Scrubbing the Sink

Yesterday, while scrubbing the sink we'd
recently bathed my infant son in to a
depthless, flawless white the chrome tap
hung across like a space vehicle (that's
the kind of thing I think about while
scrubbing sinks) it struck me: my death,
if my son holds for me what I held
for my dad, will rip the poor kid a
hole in his guts, the same as my dad's
ripped for me; and this is the cost the
love that I want now for us imposes.
Would it be better not to be beloved,
than to inflict that daily absence?
Then (this being the kind of thing
I think about while rubbing sinks)
I saw, in the dimensionless whiteness
above which flew the tap, the hole that
runs through my son's life connected
to the hole that runs through mine,
and that ran through my father's life,
and that pierced (I believe) the core of
his father's before him, all the way
back to... when? To some miserable
bastard, lost in heartlessness, whose
son shrugged off his last departure as
merely another bleak sunset, or less? Could
indifference cap such a pipe-line? Then
I thought of all that conduit might carry,
umbilical nourishment besides whatever
filth and waste, and I knew beyond doubt
it does not begin or end with me.

Love Poem (for Lisa)

Love is not blind;
love sees with subtle eyes
through our eyes, but we
do not always see what love sees.

When love moves us
we are helpless and wondering as infants.
Moving with love
we are sure and forceful as the tides.

Love seems to live
at night, in the silver surrender
of the waves, to thrive
in what shimmers darkly. But love

glints in the sand
we fill our pails with
beneath the sun, and love
lights each room of our castle.

My Essence

That moment I gave my father permission to die:
I was coming from somewhere and going to somewhere,
perhaps it was home, and it was night, that night
of May 15, the road I remember was grey and empty
passing the hospital - when was it something called me
to stop there? Was I on the interstate, or had I curved
off an exit already? The hospital was out of my way.
It was where my mother stayed all day,
by his bedside, weeks on weeks of that coma
nobody but my sister the nurse would say was final,
and she would not say that to any of us.
But memory picks me up only on that empty stretch
slowing to the entrance, the parking lot, where
something had called me. So, in my memory I am
forever answering a call, having been called, but not
in the act of being called, the moment of that is lost.
And then I am in his room. Did he have a roommate?
The other bed is empty. Why? Because I do not remember
anyone in it. And he is lying on his back, eyes closed,
the breath going in and the breath going out as if it had
nothing to do with him, every once in a while
that "aargh" from his throat around the tubes and
the cheeks flutter in and out. I watch, I want
to say something, I say something, I shut up.
Either he knows I'm here or not. Nothing special
happens, nothing that has not been happening
for weeks and weeks, breath by breath. Then his
eyelids flutter. Just a twitch at first. I watch.
All I can do is watch and wonder. Then he turns
his head, that great beak of a nose like a ship's prow
above the slack sails of his cheeks - when is the bow
higher than the canvas save when the ship is
sliding stern first down - to face me, eyelids
slowly hoisting open all this time, this infinite

time it takes to hoist his eyelids open, and all
I can do is watch and wonder. Then he gets them
open on me, the full blue as light as the band
around the horizon at noon, and holds on me
that gaze so terrible and vast in its comprehension,
so calm as cloudlessness. My heart cannot stand
within those eyes, that effort to open them, it is
too much, I babble praise of his love and beauty and
bravery and strength, stupid words borne on
a stream of liquid gold, and tell him it is okay,
he doesn't have to, he can close his eyes and rest.
And turning them to the ceiling, he does, the breath
rests. And does not come back. When I am sure
it is not coming back, I walk down the hall to the
nurse for confirmation. When she confirms that
the breath is not coming back, she leaves me alone
with the corpse. I lie across it and sob. When I rise,
it has turned orange and I am once again
in possession of and fully outside of my self.

The Potter's Death

There was a moment when the breath went out of him
not to return. His hands, useless except for
their lacework of veins that had been hooked into
the hospital's larger, cruder macrame
of tubes and bottles, for days had lain across
his chest, folded down as people do
to cast shadow silhouettes of wingless
birds - their heads and beaks - a posture almost
prayerful. More than a year before, those hands
had set aside their skill to cast his gestures
in wet clay, bathe them in fire, and turn
to stone his fingers' curving course of passage.
That tea pot. This onion-bellied vase:
I press a palm against the form's cool cheek and
feel a thing so simple I forget
the forty years of days at the whirling wheel
that rubbed his gestures clean as this, so clean.
The neck flows into the lip, a ring so small
one thumb and forefinger could have left it there.
And when his breath went out and simply failed
to come back in, that gesture seemed so easy,
as if his entire life was spent to learn it.

This poem describes a vision of death that helped me come to terms, many decades later, with the loss of my first love. In the dream, I watched her killed by a falling tree limb. In "reality," it was a car crash and I wasn't there.

Where Her Body Was

A huge limb comes crashing down...
By slow degrees, her skin turns dry
and white, so white it almost seems to glow,
as blood drains from it to pool in her back.
The sometimes quarreling, always imperious voices
that emanated from the center
of control are silent, and the great,
driving pumps of heart and lungs are
crushed and still. Without them, no supplies
arrive to replenish exhausted cells.

Uncollected, toxic wastes pile up.
Nothing comes to take them away.
Muscle fibers hook and pull together,
contracting tightly, then find they lack
the chemical energy to unhook, even
were a signal to do so to reach them.
Who would think that first among what's lost in
death is the power of relaxation? A
feral dog, worrying at the calf of
her bent leg, fails to unbend it. But

failing maintenance and replenishment, what was
fast wears out; later, when some
rats come by, her limbs respond to them.
They are not the only visitors.
Called from so far as ten miles away by
sulfides and acids she casts on the air,
blowflies, with their great, salmon eyes and

metallic body armor, lay their
clumps of eggs on wounds and other openings.
Finding refreshment in fluids exuded from

broken-down cells, they busily scrimmage for space. A
red-faced buzzard with a lovely,
white, hooked beak breaks upon her right thigh.
Meanwhile, much as a city abandoned
by its civil and military authorities
quietens briefly - empty streets and
cautious, traumatized population homebound - but
soon small riots blossom and looting as
those upon whom the engines of social control have
hitherto ground their heaviest, spring free;

so, the milliards colonizing her gut, her
lungs and interstices, whose
labor's contributions had been accepted (if
not their DNA) by the
imperial organism whose nature it was for
them to serve, no longer brought
by it the raw materials of their lives
or held back by its thriving order,
turn to take for themselves the meat that surrounds them.
So begins their time of plenty:

eating, excreting, and multiplying with
irrational exuberance;
adventuring to all corners of the realm
up arteries, veins, and lymphatic ducts
(now empty of all other moving traffic)
from which, before, they were forbidden;
mottling her pallid hide with lines and patches in
orange, red, blue-green, and
curved across her belly a streak of black: her
swelling belly. Putrescine,

cadaverine, methane, hydrogen sulfide,
ammonia, and mercaptans off-gassed by
microbes consuming carbohydrates and proteins
balloon her skin, gurgle, and blatt from
existing orifices. The trunk and limbs lose
definition of muscles and joints, grow
smoothly tubular, crude as a sock puppet.
Somewhere about what might have been the
back of the left knee, a fissure opens
in the drying, over-stretched skin and

soon it is populated by the blowflies'
teeming, tawny, voracious larvae
and the wasps and beetles that prey on them. But
now the ground around the body is
dark and soaked with its escaping juices, a
flood so rich it causes a patch of
indian pipe, already drooping, to swoon. The
desiccating tissues toughen.
Maggots drop away and creep beneath the
leaf mold, into the soil that will shelter their

own next great transformation.
Nervously glaring around between each
plunge of its sharp beak, one last raven
picks at stragglers, then hops away.
Now the death becomes so much less lively.
The residue of internal organs
uneaten by microbes, insects, birds, or beasts
turns to slush and drains away. The
leathery tatters of skin and tissue that drape the
bones are slowly picked away by

weather's prying fingers of heat and cold,
wet and dry, with now and then some
help from an occasional gnawing tooth. The
rhythm lengthens. Light and dark pass

many times across a loosening flake
before it falls or is blown away.
At last, all that's left is the denuded, intricate
web of hydroxyapatite strands and
collagen fibrils - the structure of bones. The rhythm
lengthens. Putrefaction's acid

bath already has weakened the crystals' weave.
Now, bacteria eat the proteins,
leaving gaps and channels water enters,
freezing in cracks, expanding, thawing,
trickling, leaching calcium away.
Fungi and algae take their mite.
Some time, it's impossible to say when, this
many-handed diminution
reaches the point of invisibility, and
all that I am left to look at

is a carpet of leaves, of every shade from
palest yellow to deepest chocolate,
slowly becoming soil; indian pipes
nodding; a clump of trilliums that
wasn't there before; a trail of golden
chanterelles; the oak's hard bole, where
calcium rises. Watching all this, I've felt
everything you might imagine.
In my hand, from fingertip through palm, I
feel her long and slender touch.

The Rabbit

Shaggy, ripe for mowing, backyard lawn:
it's the patch behind my house.
There in the corner's the scraggly arborvitae
overshadowed by buckthorn saplings.
Lying near it, a thing the length of my forearm, a
grey streak on the creeping charlie.
Stepping cautiously closer, I see it's a rabbit.
Why is it lying there, so still?

Then I see it's breathing, and I see the
straight, clean slash that opens its
belly front to back, revealing a jumble of
lilac, lavender, brown, and yellow
organs, still tightly packed and glistening.
Did a hawk do this, then drop you?
As I bend a little closer, you scrabble
with your stiff front legs, dragging your
shoulders to interpose your head between
me and your body, fixing on me an

eye's expressionless, dark blue bead.
I retreat to the shed for a spade to
end this misery, but, when I return, the
rabbit's dead. I bury it.
Hanging the spade back on its peg, I'm followed
by your dark blue bead
and the strength that utterly spent itself on
facing whatever I might bring you.
Gyres in darkness a bead as blue as the ocean
I face in my shock and awe.

Reincarnation
(For Jane, masseuse extraordinaire)

The last thing I felt was warmth in the middle
of my chest and a spot of it on the crown
of my head, your touch, as if your arms
ran a conduit plugging those places together;
then that was gone; my eyes were closed;
I floated in a black place. Somewhere a bone
flute knitted high and low seamless as a mitten.
I floated in my body bag, waiting for something
to return. Nothing returned. Then, as I floated,
a click from the other room, a little boy's
blocks clacked, and here a puff of breeze
on my bare chest seconded this call. So my
eyelids lightened, filled with the possibility
of motion as slowly as canal locks fill with water;
opened; and there was this glaring white blank
I recognized after a while as your ceiling and not
the eye of god because if it had been god's eye
the thoughts that kept tugging at my attention -
of the flute, of you and your husband and child,
of my wife and children, of the streets between -
would have pulled me away; but there remained
your ceiling in awesome steadfast finality.
Then you peeked in the door, quietly asking
if I was all right, and I knew it had become time,
the muscles in my limbs were mine again,
to move, pull on my shirt, and button it.

Meditation

In its ivory cage the winged dog chases
its own tail with swoops and loop-de-loops, soars
intricately at its varied paces
past the speed-blurred bars and just-ajar door.

Drugs might help you track its flight in trails that
curlicue and dash with almost meaning,
weaving finer than the Book of Kells. But
this once, at the door, it stops careening,

pokes a quivering snout outside - *The air hums.*
Sheets of scent it had torn through now stretch un-
ending, undulating, full of what comes to
he who waits. The seconds slowly stretch. - then,

fearing immense spaces unflapped by dogwings
snaps back to embroidering its nothings.

Udrak, a virtuoso of meditation, was one of the Buddha's early mentors. As with all his other teachers, Buddha understood something about the practice that Udrak did not.

The Song of Udrak

Master meditator, you who
fixed your mind upon the pearl indenting
your pure brow and breathed its coolness,
changeless, unwound all the ragged flags of
thought to blow in nothing's breezes,
watched the lion's mane stir slow as
blades of grass, and all the while your

shaven head became unshaved, the stubble
grey, a million grey births boiling
from your scalp, and elongating greyly
dawn and noon and dusk and night.
Dawn and noon and dusk and night they grew,
a million grey births aging, while you
sat somewhere behind your eyeballs, taking
it all in and breathing out, and
breathing in and out. The mice had long since
learned to dance across your thighs, your

imperturbed and folded limbs their runways,
when their cousin rats moved in and
added yet another set of accents
to the polyrhythmic scurry.
Bolder, they would climb your form, their claws find
purchase on you, trigger nerves each
dawn and noon and dusk and night. Dawn and
noon and dusk and night they grow, a
million grey births aging, while you note
unmoved each prickling passing. Motes of

dust show where the air moves. Voices great and
small; all sorts of birds and bugs; the
sunlight's slide across the floor; the hiss and
creak, inaudible, of leaves and
stems that follow it; rain's varied kisses,
also wind's; the pulse of day, and
night's expanse - all weave the web in which
abides your calm awareness, wakeful,
resting as if in a hammock, dawn and
noon and dusk and night. Dawn and

noon and dusk and night it grows, a million
grey births aging. Then, at last
acceding to an itch, you know it's time to
stop, to start again. You rise like
steam, and walking past a window see
reflected havoc that the rats gnawed in
your hair. Your anger soars. But later,
standing over several still-warm,
long-tailed corpses, you recall that wide-eyed
vision ghosting on the glass, and

there's an inkling, so uneasy: one may
have his feelings without being had by
them, each dawn and noon and dusk and night.
Dawn and noon and dusk and night they
stir, a million grey waves, cresting, falling.

Fable

There were Words that could look behind Themselves.
Whatever They saw would shine from Their foreheads:
      green stalks of unmowed grass,
      a trout's scales losing color beside the stream,
      a young person's indecision about love,
      clouds snagged on mountains.

You could not look such a Word in the eye
unless you were willing to let It turn your
hair white and make you talk with a stutter,
leaving you youthful and fluent only when
your own mouthful of significant noises
acknowledged It as mother and father.

That worked until for reasons beyond my scope
people mostly forgot the other side of their heads,
where the Words flitted in and out like bluebirds
with big foreheads. Into the black, blank orbs of
Their eyes almost no one remembered
how to look or why someone might want to.

But then there were just these foreheads floating around
in a forward-looking world becoming ever more so,
increasingly confident where its next step might lead
because there undeniably in plain sight were its toes.

People paid to fit the young into boxes asked:
      What does a stalk of grass signify?
      Why did the trout's scales lose their color?
      Why can't she make up his mind?
      What does it mean to snag a cloud?
The young decided anything would be more fun
than staring into those gleaming, pitiless foreheads.

Now the Words hang out in bars, grown smaller
than hummingbirds; hovering almost weightless
for the chance to dart into a surprise
unmonetized silent moment and suck its
nectar before hissing espresso machines and the
room's low mutter of romantic confusion
blow them away; hesitating; losing color.

Peony

Every morning begins with a song
I am practicing but can't yet sing
nor ever will be able to capture
perfectly that last phrase's
seamless bass to falsetto run
the way my teacher showed me
saying "you are not as I am"
but "practice anyway" and yet
despite the breaks and squeaks
every failure makes me
smile my teacher said the song's
a petal fallen from the peony
that blooms above your head
every day a petal fallen
from the peony that blooms

The Dragon of Sassafras Mountain

My mother told me this story when I was little. I wanted to write it down for years - decades, really - and finally did it in 1996, when I was forty-four and had two young children, eight and five years old, about the same age that I had been. For some reason, getting my mother to tell it to them was not an option, although she had about ten years left to live. I seem to recall that, when asked, she said she didn't remember the story. That's quite possible. My mother was a vastly creative, deeply introverted person in charge of three small children at the time she made it up. She was perfectly capable of spinning off a tale that one of them would remember for the rest of his life, although to her its significance in the moment might have been only as the means of obtaining respite from demands for amusement. One way or another, it was up to me to pass it on.

When spring's last frost glazed greening grass,
The King and Queen decided at last:

Their daughter, just grown five years old,
Was so bold that she should be told

To STAY OUT OF THE MOAT, where floated
Lily pads, gold fish, and bloated

Frogs. And why? BECAUSE, they firmly
Instructed the Princess sitting squirmy

On her tuffet, A CURSE WAS LAID
UPON THOSE WATERS. "What?" the maid

Inquired, wide-eyed and erect. "What curse?"
"To keep invaders out, and worse,"

Replied her dad, "they hired a witch
When the moat was dug to smite that ditch.

What the curse was, I don't know.
But surely, it's there. We've told you so."

"Yes, sure it is," she smiled right back,
"And now can I go get my snack?"

They nodded yes, but then she frowned
And asked, as her slippers touched the ground,

"What could be worse than awful invaders?"
"A princess wading without her waders,"

Quickly interjected the Queen.
"Worser than anything you've ever seen?"

"Don't joke!" said her dad with a catch in his throat,
"And DON'T LET US CATCH YOU NEAR THE MOAT."

But, when summer dazed the nodding flowers
And bees danced doggedly beneath castle towers,

Tall, cool spears in the still, hot air,
Of course, you know what's next, how fair

Princess Isabella dove
Head-first off the drawbridge and strove

To split the surface, smooth and green,
Dotted with water-lilies, just between

Two of the largest lily pads,
Where frogs sat, sunning. Her mom and dad

Were sweating in the kitchen, planning
Their daughter's birthday bash, so, banning

Thoughts of them from mind, the Princess,
Not even pausing to undress,

Savored the swish into darkness beneath
Her splash, her slide through the liquid sheath,

Lily leaves' brush against her toes,
Bubbles glubbing from her nose.

After a while it got kind of boring.
She climbed to her room and soon was snoring

Sprawled across her bed, her hair
And clothes still damp, her fine feet bare.

Those toes might have pointed up forever.
"Call Isabella! I want to have her

Down here at once!" the Queen exclaimed
When dinner had passed and dessert came

Riding on its silver wheels
Without the Princess. "Missing meals

Is not okay!" A maid-in-waiting
Hurried forth and returned, stating,

"She's sleeping upstairs, sound as a lamb."
"Well, let her," the King said, spooning jam.

"Tomorrow she'll wake quite ravenous.
Tomorrow, her birthday, there'll be such a fuss,

She'll need all the rest she can get today.
Would you pass one of those tarts my way?"

But when her birthday through she slumbered,
Even the King's aplomb was encumbered.

It rained that day, and as he bent
To follow closely her breath as it went

Out then in, he also heard
A liquid sound, that somehow pattered

Around his heart to form a shallow
Pool; within which limply rose to

Float an image: a sun-frocked child
Who had been vibrant, bright, and wild.

The Queen thrice said to him, "My dear,"
Before he thought to turn to her.

She reined her panic. "Perhaps we
Should ask the Doctor what she sees?"

"Yes." He recovered. "Or should we wait?
She's much less trouble in this state."

But "lying in state" came to his mind,
His father recently having declined

From throne to bed to marble box
To be adored by weeping flocks.

He added, "I'm sure she'll be all right."
Enter the Doctor, a mild, shy light

Of empathy playing about her lips
Otherwise pursed to withhold tips

From those too ill or weak or concerned
To handle what she knew. She'd learned

To seem as vague as if dappled in shade.
Silvery-greyish hair curls strayed

Loose from her hat to her furrowed brow,
The floppy-broad brim secured by a bow

Tied beneath her dimpled chin.
The Doctor, like the King, leaned in.

She drew a breath, and leaned far back.
Just at that moment, clip-clop, clack,

Clattering boots rushed in from the hall.
A muddy Gardener hailed them all.

The flustered Doctor, wheeling around,
Exclaimed at this distracting sound.

The Gardener hollered, "Her sandals! We've found them!
Oh, pardon me." The Doctor: "Ahem...

Well, hand them here... Let me see...
Where did you find them?" "In the lea

'Twixt moat and castle, 'midst buttercups."
A faint smile grazed the dreaming lips,

Unnoticed. The Doctor frowned. "You found
Them on the moat-bank, or on level ground?"

"Just near the top, where the moat begins."
The King held the Queen as she drew in

A shaking draught of the air of that room,
Its dust-and-lilacs tinge, slow doom

She'd not until that moment scented.
"Medicine, I think, has not invented

What may be needed here," the Physician
Drawled. "Perhaps the Court Magician

Will know what to do. Call the man
In the tall, cone hat! Look elsewhere than

My humble science, m'lord and lady.
Reality's darkened by something shady,

That's what I think. I know what she's not:
Asleep, or drugged, or playing a part,

Or comatose... For better or worse,
You might best treat this as a curse.

You might ask, could there be worse news?
But what thing doesn't demand its dues?

What I, a doctor of physic, can't cure,
Or may not heal but with far more

Of pain and loss than illness caused,
May be amenable to other laws

That properly banish it with a snap!"
Summoned, he came with a sprightly step,

The Palace Mage. A long, blue cape,
Suitably speckled with stars, was draped

Around his narrow shoulders and fluttered
Down to his ankles. The words he uttered

Were few and to the point. "Hello.
It's her? I see." He bent her toe

Between a thumb and bony forefinger
Lightly, let it go, and watched it linger

Where he'd left it then slowly straighten.
"Moat," he murmured, then, "This maiden

Needs a cup of tea. That's all."
The King spun, shouting down the hall,

"Water! Heat some - " "Not so fast.
Not <u>any</u> tea. Just sassafras."

"I'm sure cook's got that in the larder,"
breathed the Queen. The King yelled harder,

"Brew us up a pot of - " "Nope.
Only on the lower slopes

Of Sassafras Mountain grow the trees
Whose root bark, shaved fine, is what you need.

Stuff from hereabouts?! Might as well
Fill a bucket from a dry well."

The darkness in the hall behind him
Seemed to part like curtains of scrim

For the passage of a presence
Whose entrance commanded a hush, and incense

Mustily weighed in their noses. A hairless
Head atop black robes smiled cheerily

At them from the corridor, dripping
Sweat and panting. "My friend," he said, gripping

The King's right hand. "Yes, here I am.
In your need, so glad that I am

Here to give aid! Say what it is
This humble subject can give of his

To succor the sweet dear princessling!
Oh, anything at all! Yes, anything! Anything!"

Earnestly looking the King in the eyes.
"Um... well, yes... that is, I'm surprised..."

His Majesty mumbled. "Oh, kind High Priest,"
The Queen added nimbly, "There's not the least - "

"Of course there is! Not man nor beast
Shall stand in the way of my serving the least

Of your needs that the Spirit of Healing"
(Here he cast his gaze up at the ceiling)

"Bids me serve. To the greater glory
Of the Power we follow, my offertory

Is this: for you, this I will do:
I'll go to the Sassafras Mountain for you!"

The startled Queen: "But, how did you know - "
The Mage "The walls have ears." "Just so,"

The High Priest chuckled, as the King glanced about
As if to see what the walls would sprout.

"Well, fine then. Great! I don't mean to be rude.
This is happening so fast. My gratitude

Will ripen more sweetly," said the King, with calm
freshly cloaked, "when you bring us this balm."

Making a show of high humility
Was the Priest's most famous ability.

He rode next morning, his helpful mission
Cheered by thousands early arisen

On churchly orders to line the battlements
With song and trumpets and colorful pennants.

With hopeful thunder they urged him on
Squat on his donkey, into the dawn.

He ambled down the dusty road
So peacefully as if to goad

The crowds to greater encouragement,
Then disappeared around a bend

And never was seen in that land again.
They waited and waited, the King and the Queen,

And waited and waited and waited some more,
While, slumbering so deep not even a snore

Troubled her nose, the Princess lay pale
And sweet as a rose. When six weeks failed

The Priest's return, they gave him up
For good. "Lost for a simple cup

Of tea!" the Queen, eyes brimming, mourned.
"Such sentiments should not be scorned,"

Rejoined His Honor the Lord Mayor,
At lunch with the Queen so as to convey her

His public's deepest condolences.
His small eyes cast their sharp, quick glances

First at the Mage, then at the Princess.
"At such a time of deep distress

They cast a light of nobleness
On you, Poor Madam. I'm impressed!"

With this, he shrugged and gestured wide
As if to show he could not hide,

Even beneath his meaty shoulders,
His admiration from any beholders.

"Not so simple," muttered the Mage,
Who never liked to be upstaged,

But they ignored him. "That's nice," said the King,
"But nice words don't much do anything."

"And that is why, sires, sir and ma'am,
I have prepared an action plan

Whereby the people of this great city
May demonstrate their love and pity

And, with a little help from me,
Procure your daughter her cup of tea!

Now, pray don't ask me to reveal
The details. Not that I'd conceal

The smallest matter from your eyes;
Just let this be a grand surprise.

I ask permission, not for me,
But for your adoring citizenry,

Whose servant I am, to bestow this boon,
And, by your leave, you'll have it soon!"

Whatever excitement the Mayor might stir
In the lower ranks, it was quite sure

He'd never given his lord and liege
Cause to shout. "Go, lay seige

To the Sassafras Mountain however you wish,"
The King dismissed with a nod and a swish

Of the hand; the Queen likewise, eyes blank.
Expecting nothing, they murmured their thanks.

They waited a few more dreary weeks
While through their capitol's shops and streets

There hummed the web of protegés, cronies
Toadies, flunkies, and ambitious phonies

That vibrated at the Mayor's pluck
And fixed the odds to try his luck.

Come the big day, a flock of white birds
Was loosed and chased by stirring words.

Bands played, a hundred vendors hawked
Their sausages and drinks, and speakers squawked

One after another to oblivious crowds
Of "historic times" and how they were proud.

At last, some constables tried to part
The milling mob so the Mayor could start,

With no more effect than a stick drawn through sand;
Right behind them, it closed up again.

More cops, batons drawn ready to strike,
Formed a line and made it a dike

Behind which passed the Mayor, his crew,
And scrivening journalists, two by two,

All the party of power and renown,
Bejeweled, beribboned, bedecked, begowned

As if for a formal country picnic.
The Mayor paused to utter a quick

Goodbye to those on whose behalf
He hoped, he said with a modest laugh,

To soon take the credit of finding the cure.
Then off they went, and were seen no more

Except for one who, three weeks later,
Tottered home, her clothes all tattered,

Out of breath and empty of hand,
So tired and scared she barely could stand,

A former Assistant to the Very
Honorable Under Secretary.

Herewith her report: "It was so sunny,
There on that meadow, and breezy, that many

Left the road and romped in the grass
While others went to collect sassafras

From trees that covered the nearby hill
With baskets and bags they were ordered to fill

As full as they could and only to stop
When they'd enough to stock all our shops

With sprigs to sell as souvenirs
Of the Mayor's Crusade. They were volunteers.

I can't say who. I hung back, lazy,
Beneath a tree, admiring a daisy."

She paused and bit her lip, and went on.
"And now they are all, everyone, gone."

Tears and a sip of brandy, more tears.
Wiping her nose with her wrist: "One hears

Of such things, but I... well... there was
That ring of white petals, that yellow fuzz,

And suddenly a sound like grating granite,
And all of those poor people ran at

Me, at the road... were licked away
By drooling flame tongues. They turned grey

And crumbled on the horrid wind...
Only the tree I stood behind

Blackened, but shielded only me.
Behind the fire strode something green."

Then she could speak no more. They led her,
Sobbing, to the kitchen, where they fed her.

After a while, the Magician spoke.
"The Dragon... I'd thought it was a joke..."

"What?!" snapped the King. "How can this be?"
"A story my teacher passed on to me

Of a fire breathing lizard that guards that hill,
I thought in jest." "You miserable fool!"

No," said the Queen, "look. He's not sad.
Almost the only rivals he had

For your ear, my dear, have met their last woes.
It's no joke. Nothing he knows

Has ever been a joke." "Get out!"
The King in anguish thundered. "Out!

Get out of my home and out of my palace,
You scheming, conjuring bag of malice!"

"But he told us the cure for our daughter,"
The Queen said, her voice as clear as water,

"And surely that deserves our love."
She spoke as if that were what she was full of,

So the King would be drawn to drink of it, too.
"Never again will I listen to you

Without listening twice," he said softly. "Stay,
Then. Putter about here, out of my way,

In the back halls where mice creep and bats
Make droppings, and count your blessings that

I do not put you to my own
Hot fires." So made his exit the Magician,

After bowing and saying, "Madame,
I will not forget how I am

Indebted to your truthful kindness."
But, that's another story. Blindness

Of hopelessness then ate them both, the parents
Whose child would not awaken to stir and

Grow. They moped and lived their days
By rote and their sleep was like a daze.

Then, that winter, when ice like iron
Banded all the roads, and crying

High, the winds bored every hole
And played each eave a tuneless whistle,

The Captain of the Guard arose
From his oaken desk, slapped closed

The pile of files that he'd been reading,
Paused to think, pivoted, and treading

Swiftly and heavily through the halls,
Entered the throne room before the calls

Of heralds could announce him.
Torches unlit, the place was dim.

The King was planted on his throne,
Listlessly answering "yes" or "no"

To things that pages read from pages.
In a voice that could cut through rages

Of battle to burnish his soldiers' purpose,
"I can do it, and I propose

You let me," the Captain declared. Aroused,
The King surveyed the figure which housed

His reign's main muscle. Elegantly
Tailored silk, his suit but scantly

Seemed to contain his barrel chest
And stumpy legs. His face expressed

The simpler feelings, strongly; blank,
This moment, an idling battle tank;

With eyes of grey that never let
Out what they let in, nothing let

Escape. The King remembered
How the Princess, last December,

Frolicked before those eyes, those arms
That, folded across his chest, did harm

To the seams of their sleeves. He asked, "Do what?"
"Slay the beast and seize the root.

The Dragon Unit was disbanded
Long ago, but training is standard.

I've updated the *Manual
Of Weapons and Tactics.* The *Annual

Digest of Major Lizard Sightings*
For your grandfather's reign gives fighting

Tips, like how to couch your lance.
That salamander's got no chance!"

"All right," said the King, recalling how
Seldom the Captain indulged in bravado;

That last claim had been one of fact.
"Do it. I thank you for the act

Before it's done. Now go. I'm tired."
For even hope was a burden, required

More will to suffer than he had.
In this, the mom was like the dad.

Numbly, next morning, the royals stood
Atop the battlements and watched a flood

Of motley celebrants pour through the gate
Behind a black war steed, sedate

With its terrible, weaponed rider, whose glance
Was something from which they kept their distance

And slowly, smoothly fell behind.
Swiftness often brings to mind

How swiftly comes the stop. Slow seems
More unrelenting, eternal as dreams.

So he advanced towards the fatal hill.
They watched him dwindle with distance until

The gate thud shut below and cut
The chain that held their eyes. Now what

They did was wait. A few days later
Arrived a crumpled, travel-stained letter

From, of all people, the former Priest,
Confessing that he'd run from a Beast

That he, after months of agonized
Soul-searching, at last now realized

It would be wrongful not to reveal
Was a dragon, despite the shame he'd feel.

He begged forgiveness, liege sirrah,
Et cetera, et cetera.

Then, nothing. A few more seasons, days
And nights, and meals, and time that lays

Between the things one does, and time
That one spends doing them, and time

Asleep. The King and Queen began
To lose their memories of when

Their daughter's life was fully lived
Together with them, and to revive

Some of their pleasure in each other;
For which, unspoken guilt now bothered

Them, somewhat. Their smiles stayed shy
And few. And then, one springtime day,

A wandering scholar knocked at the gate.
Saying, "I hope I am not too late,"

He waved a fistful of blackish shreds
Of something at the Gatekeeper, said,

"This may interest the royal family,
Or so I'm informed - botanically,

S. officinale, though medically,
Magnolia glauca or nectandra puchury

Or even atherosperma moschata
Might serve as well; the latter is not a

Species indigenous to these climes - "
The Gatekeeper almost rang his chimes

With his poleaxe before he understood,
Then hustled the fellow and his bits of wood

(Still yakking) to the kitchen, where
A steaming kettle was promptly prepared.

A dollop of tisane produced from the Princess
A mighty splutter. Despite the mess,

They poured in a cup, and were joyous to get
Her risen from bedclothes soaking wet.

Much later, after linens were changed,
And clothes, and celebrations arranged,

And hugs, and grins, and whoops, and cheers,
And eyes were bleary with happy years,

The King and Queen took the scholar aside
And asked, "How did you do it? Confide!"

"We scholars are a wandering lot.
Classes had ended, and I thought,

Before I accepted a new teaching post
I'd travel wherever it pleased me the most.

I saddled my donkey, packed light for summer,
And hit the road. I had read somewhere

Of rare volumes that might be found
In a barn in one of your northern towns,

Property of a gentleman farmer.
Now, I do not mean to alarm or

Otherwise perturb you, but
Your kingdom's libraries are not

Well stocked with basic source texts in
My field, a shame, considering...

But I digress. He shared my field,
This learned plowman. His barn would yield

Me months of study, free from all pester,
All summer through to the autumn semester.

A rural idyll! During the trip
I sat my donkey and idly flipped

Through a recent treatise or two,
And, I almost blush to tell you,

That fat new romance by what's-his-name,
The man with the beard, about how fame

And fortune proved someone's downfall.
I can't recall their names at all,

Author or hero. About page three
Hundred or so, I felt a wee

Bit thirsty. The back of my throat was dry.
A burning smell and the sun in the sky

Became more than vague sensations.
I lowered my book. The situation

That met my eyes was rather strange.
I saw a barren hill, the range

Between its slopes and my road quite littered
With fallen, burnt black trees. There glittered

Near the horizon, something. I squinted
Towards it - the air was hazy, tinted

Smoky blue - and barely could discern
Two tiny, distant figures stirring

Up a cloud of soot and dust,
Circling, lunging, parry and thrust,

Fighting, in a word, a knight
And a great, green, scaly thing, and fight

And fight they did as dusk now leached
Away the light. My tired eyes reached

Their limits. The last I saw, his sword
Was silhouetted on flames which poured

As if from nothing, going nowhere.
My donkey nuzzled a charred root, there

By the side of the road. I pulled it loose,
Identified it - sassafras -

And thought, how nice to have some tea.
So, I brought it along with me.

A few hours later, there twinkled ahead
The kitchen light of my farmstead.

But, they wouldn't let me stay!
One look at my root and they sent me away

To here. I admit, it took some urging.
I had not known that you were searching

For this botanical remedy.
A dragon, you know, is like a bee,"

He mused, "If you don't bother it,
Well, it won't bother you." "That's it?!"

The King and Queen exclaimed. It was.
By noon next day, the streets were abuzz

With workers massing hastily
To build the scholar a library

With all the tomes that he could name.
From opening day, he never came

Out again. The humbug Priest
Lived on, alone with memories.

And the Captain and dragon, by their scorched hill,
Clashed ever more fiercely, and fight there still.

Acknowledgements

"Five Year Old Wins Fishing Derby" was published in *The Sow's Ear Poetry Review*, Vol. VI, No. 1 (July 1995).

"My Essence" was published in *Hunger Mountain, The Vermont College Journal of Arts and Letters*, Spring 2004 Issue.

Several poems appearing her are excerpted from *In Dante's Wake*, a trilogy by Seth Steinzor. "Where Her Body Was" is from *Among the Lost* (Fomite Press 2016). "The Rabbit" is from *Once Was Lost* (Fomite Press 2021). "The Song of Udrak" is from *To Join the Lost* (Antrim House 2010, reissued by Fomite Press 2016).

About the Author

Seth Steinzor was born seven years after the Holocaust, beginning the third generation in America of a Jewish family with a history of atheism, socialism, and labor organizing. He spent his childhood in the suburbs of Buffalo, New York, during the years of the Civil Rights Movement, the Kennedy assassination, Israel's triumph in the Six Day War, and America's plunge into degradation in Vietnam. These were the significant events in forming his political consciousness. His parents, craftspeople and teachers, encouraged his creativity, which primarily took the form of considerable verbal precocity.

Graduating from Middlebury College in 1974, Steinzor hung about town for a while. A job with the local Public Defender led him to three years of misery at the University of Maine Law School. Escaping with his Juris Doctor degree in 1979, he did not put it to use until 1990, when he was appointed an Assistant Attorney General for the State of Vermont, having spent the previous five years investigating employment discrimination claims for the Vermont Attorney General's Office Civil Rights Division. For the next twenty-seven years, he represented the State in various capacities. In the meantime he married, fathered two children, divorced, and wrote most of *In Dante's Wake*. He retired from the Attorney General's Office and from the law in 2017, to a life of writing, woodworking, gardening, music making, and voracious reading.

Fomite

Writing a review on social media sites for readers will help the progress of independent publishing. To submit a review, go to the book page on any of the sites and follow the links for reviews. Books from independent presses rely on reader-to-reader communications.

For more information or to order any of our books, visit:
http://www.fomitepress.com/our-books.html

More poetry from Fomite...
Anna Blackmer — *Hexagrams*
L. Brown — *Loopholes*
Sue D. Burton — *Little Steel*
Christine Butterworth-McDermott — *Evelyn As*
Christine Butterworth-McDermott — *The Spellbook of Fruit and Flowers*
David Cavanagh— *Cycling in Plato's Cave*
Rajnesh Chakrapani — *The Repetition of Exceptional Weeks*
James Connolly — *Picking Up the Bodies*
Benjamin Dangl — *A World Where Many Worlds Fit*
Greg Delanty — *Behold the Garden*
Greg Delanty — *Loosestrife*
Mason Drukman — *Drawing on Life*
J. C. Ellefson — *Foreign Tales of Exemplum and Woe*
Anna Faktorovich — *Improvisational Arguments*
Peter Fortunato — *World Headquarters*
Barry Goldensohn — *Snake in the Spine, Wolf in the Heart*
Barry Goldensohn — *The Hundred Yard Dash Man*
Barry Goldensohn — *The Listener Aspires to the Condition of Music*
Barry Goldensohn — *Visitors Entrance*
Lorrie Goldensohn — *Little Fish*
R. L. Green — *When You Remember Deir Yassin*
KJ Hannah Greenberg — *Beast There—Don't That*
Kevin Hadduck — *Beloved Brother, Beloved Sister*
John Hawkins — *Mirror to Mirror*
Christopher Heffernan — *[laughter]*
Gail Holst-Warhaft — *Lucky Country*
Judith Kerman — *Definitions*
Yahia Lababidi — *Quarantine Notes*
Joseph Lamport — *Enlightenment*
Raymond Luczak — *A Babble of Objects*
Kate Magill — *Roadworthy Creature, Roadworthy Craft*
Tony Magistrale — *Entanglements*
Gary Mesick — *General Discharge*
Giorigio Mobili — *Sunken Boulevards*

Fomite

www.ingramcontent.com/pod-product-compliance
Lightning Source LLC
Chambersburg PA
CBHW031447120626
46545CB00006B/2584